TELL YOUR STORY

Sharing your faith

with confidence

Gordon Moore

CONTENTS

INTRODUCTION

The reason for the original writing of this book came from the need in our church for practical material to help our church members connect more effectively with their unchurched family, friends and colleagues.

It seems as though the 'Great Commission' has become the 'Great Omission', relegating evangelism to the domain of the few - those bold, outgoing, always-making-friends-of-everyone kind of people who seem to be so able to naturally share their faith. In turn, we continue on with our lives, putting evangelism in the 'too hard basket' because to try means certain failure.

But this is not the way it has to be! I have good news!

'The few' will always be good at 'confrontational evangelism', and we need them to be! It's their gift. But for most of us, there is a way to discover how we can introduce our friends, associates and relatives to Christ as we live our daily lives.

"So what 'Evangelism Program' are you offering?" You may ask. None! That's right, none!

Here's what I've discovered; Evangelism is not a program! Evangelism is primarily a lifestyle.

TO LEAD PEOPLE TO JESUS IS PRIMARILY A LIFESTYLE

This book is written with the genuine desire to help the 'ungifted evangelists' like you and me to relax and be 'natural Christians', who, through living the life of Christ confidently every day among our friends, associates and relatives, can see them discover what we have received; God's free gift of salvation.

ENJOY!

Gordon Moore
AUTHOR

CHAPTER ONE:

THE 'E' WORD

It's a fact: we all cringe at the mention of it, the request for it, and the challenge for more of it. Yes, most of us are not effective at the 'E word', Evangelism.

But there's good news for you and me. Winning people to Jesus is not about a program, an event, or a method. It is about you and me bringing our friends, relatives and associates to Christ through the way we live, and by telling our story and presenting the Gospel.

We're Not All 'Evangelists'

Have you ever wondered why sharing Jesus seems so easy for some Christians, and yet so difficult for most?

After 45 years of active involvement in all kinds of endeavors sharing Jesus to those who haven't met Him yet, I have come to several conclusions.

Firstly, I am not a gifted evangelist, yet I have had the privilege of leading thousands of people to Christ through my ministry and leadership context, but not on my own!

Secondly, most Christians are just the same as me; they're not 'evangelists', but they can learn how to lead people to Christ through the witness of their personal lives and story.

Peter Wagner, in his book "Your Church Can Grow" (p.25), supports this concept and actually puts forward the concept that "in the average evangelical church, ten percent of the members have been given the gift of evangelism."

What a relief! I'm convinced that the pressure felt by so many Christians is the result of being sold the idea that we must all be 'evangelists'. That is, we must all be out there speaking to anyone and everyone on the street, at work, at the beach etc. with the claims of the Gospel and leading people to Christ every day.

However, this is simply not the way it is. We are not all 'evangelists', but we are all 'witnesses'.

> "But you shall receive power, after the Holy Spirit is come upon you: and **YOU SHALL BE WITNESSES** unto me…" (Acts 1:8)

I believe that making this distinction between being an 'evangelist' or a 'witness' is important, especially for our sanity and the way we go about witnessing for Christ.

There are multiple types of Evangelism

Understanding this concept is crucial to releasing effective evangelism through the church.

In the New Testament we see three types of Evangelism:

1. **'EVANGELISTS'**
2. **'PERSONAL EVANGELISTS'**
3. **'THE WORK OF AN EVANGELIST'**

The Evangelist

Phillip, the 'Evangelist', went to Samaria and won the whole city to Christ (Acts 8:5-6) and then led the Ethiopian diplomat to Christ in the desert (Acts 8:21). This is the Leadership gift mentioned in Ephesians chapter four.

The Personal Evangelist

Andrew, the 'Personal Evangelist', brought Peter his brother to Jesus. John 1:44 also links Philip with Andrew. Some have called people like Andrew the 'silent workers' because they are often unseen by most and work one on one with many people, introducing them to Christ.

The Work of an Evangelist

Timothy, the 'Pastor', not the evangelist, was encouraged by Paul to "**do the work of an evangelist**". Even though Timothy's primary gifts and focus would have been pastoring, teaching and leading the local church at Ephesus, Paul was emphatic to point out that evangelism must be at the forefront and a provision of Christian ministry – "*make full proof of your ministry*". The NET and WEB translations clarify the sense of this instruction by adding "and":

> *"But watch in all things, endure afflictions,*
> ***do the work of an evangelist****, make full*
> *proof of your ministry." (II Timothy 4:5 NET)*

> *"Do the work of an evangelist **and** fulfill your*
> *ministry." (II Timothy 4:5 WEB)*

Therefore, Paul is directly linking the "fulfillment" of Christian leadership and ministry with "the work of an evangelist".

In other words, the central focus and goal of all Holy Spirit anointed ministry is working for the saving of lost people. This is bonefide Christian ministry.

> *"Go and make disciples of all nations, baptizing*
> *them in the name of the Father, the Son and the*
> *Holy Spirit, teaching them to observe all things that*
> *I commanded you." (Matthew 28:19-20)*

Most incidents of evangelism in the New Testament are about ordinary Christians doing the 'work of an evangelist' as they went about their everyday lives. For example, Philip (a different man to the 'Evangelist' Phillip) did the "**work of an evangelist**" when he said "Come and See", and invited Nathaniel, his friend, to meet Jesus (John 1:45-46).

In the early church, conversions occurred daily in the context of the 'normal' lives of the Christians:

"Praising God, and having favour with all the people. And the Lord added to the church daily those who were being saved." (Acts 2:42)

"Therefore they that were scattered abroad went everywhere preaching the word." (Acts 8:4)

We have discovered that when we view evangelism like this, we can all be involved in reaching the unchurched with the Gospel.

Spot The Evangelist

Over the years that I've been a Christian, I've had the privilege of having friends and associates who are 'evangelists'. You can easily spot them. For example, once when I went out to a restaurant with an evangelist friend, half way through the meal, he was leading the waiter to Christ! All I wanted was to eat a meal!

Those with the gift of evangelism are specially anointed to introduce people to Christ, and they do so on a regular basis. Two members in our church for example, lead over fifty people to Christ in one year…each!

On one occasion, one of our evangelists turned up to Church with a row of new converts, all of them primed and ready to make a public commitment to Christ after my preaching.

But where does this leave you and me?

The Big Question: How do we mobilize the ninety percent?

This is what this book is all about.

The practice of effective evangelism has almost been lost to the church. According to the National Church Life Survey, the average size of a Pentecostal church in Australia is around 130 members, with 57 members in mainstream churches. More than half of all congregations in Australia have fewer than 50 attendees, and yet around 49% of church attendees feel at ease about 'sharing their faith'. Somehow there seems to be a gap between willingness and effectiveness.

Evangelism in the Bible is about ordinary people living out the call of Christ and communicating Him to non-Christians in their own environment.

This is where we derive the term "**LIFESTYLE EVANGELISM**".

Unhealthy Methods of Evangelism

Church health and growth experts agree that while some churches fail to grow because they do not evangelise, others fail to grow because they do – with irrelevant forms of communication.

Three examples of ineffective styles of evangelism are given by Joseph Aldrich in his book, "Lifestyle Evangelism":

"The Big Fisherman"

This is where the pastor of the church is perceived as 'the fisherman', with the church members as the 'inviters'. This usually results in the pastor 'evangelising the evangelised' week after week in church services and events that are geared for and attended by church members only.

"The Ambush Method"

This is where an un-churched friend is invited to a high-powered event, leaving him or her feeling trapped and cornered. This method has been aptly termed 'Evangelical Mugging'.

"The Spiritual Safari"

This is the most common method Christians understand as 'Evangelism', where Christians are exposed to confrontational styled evangelism in 'enemy territory'. This usually takes the form of street preaching and witnessing, tract distribution, and door knocking to complete strangers at home and abroad.

Research reveals that none of these methods are really fruitful in terms of effectively bringing large numbers of people to Christ and linking them into Church membership. These kind of approaches and methods tend to overlook the most important statement that Jesus made about evangelism; *"You shall **BE** witnesses unto me." (Acts 1:8)*.

To '**BE**' a witness daily to those people in my life is totally different to '**DOING**' witnessing to complete strangers!

Facing the facts

If these methods are largely ineffective, why do Christians persist with such unfruitful forms of witnessing? This is a relevant question and worth asking ourselves.

This is the point I'm making… **Witnessing is all about lifestyle**.

"Let your light so shine before men, that they may see your good works and glorify your Father in heaven." (Matthew 5:16)

Cultural Barriers and Belief Systems

The Church's culture and belief systems can also be counter-productive to evangelism.

In his book, Joseph Aldrich observes that:

"... it is fair to say that the majority of Christians have lost their ability to relate significantly to non-Christians... frequently the unsaved are viewed as the enemy rather than victims of the enemy. The new Christian is told he has 'nothing in common' with his unsaved associates. Quite frankly, I have a lot in common with them: a mortgage, car payments, kids who misbehave... It is well to remember that Jesus was called the 'friend of the sinners'. Selah!"

"Lifestyle Evangelism" by Joseph Aldrich (p.19)

The important thing to remember is that most non-Christians observe the way we **act**, **respond and treat people**, and often make their decision about Christianity based on what they **see** in our lives.

Asking the Right Questions

The questions we should be asking ourselves are; "Am I joyful, positive and stable? Do my finances demonstrate the blessing of God? Is my home life working? What kind of person am I? Instead of: "Have I memorised enough Scripture? Do I have the right tract? What if they ask me about evolution?"

People are seeing God through me

The core of evangelism is modeling what I possess in Christ and then explaining how I came to possess it. It is easier to study, comprehend and discuss truth than to be truth.

There are five Gospels: Matthew, Mark, Luke, John, and you and me. The problem is that non-Christians only read you and me.

**WE ARE LIVING EPISTLES...
BIBLE TRANSLATORS TO THE UNSAVED**

New Converts: The Life Blood of the Church

A few years ago I made this statement to our church: "The future of our church is not in here, that is, among our existing members, it is 'out there' in our unchurched community".

How true this is! If Churches fail to grow by conversions, they will die on their feet.

So much time, money and effort in churches can be put into the attracting, comforting and keeping of the saved. Our church in Brisbane has grown into a large church by mainly mobilising our members. We use online advertising from time to time for special conferences and events, but there is simply no substitute for a **mobilised membership** who are out in the community, living Christ and sharing the good news everyday, introducing their family, friends and colleagues to church and to Jesus Christ.

The result of a bias and focus towards the maintenance of the saved will result in no lasting health and growth in churches. I believe it is essential to move the focus off attracting and comforting existing Christians and church members, and onto equipping our members for the mission of the church; to reach unchurched people.

"Go and make disciples..." (Matthew 28:19)

New Converts are good for us

Our churches need new Christians because **New Converts keep us real and honest**. New Christians protect us from becoming religious because they don't understand the impractical and complicated terminology and traditions that the church can easily acquire as a result of being divorced from the real world in which we live.

New Converts force us to be open to new relationships. A constant stream of new converts coming into our churches means that we all have to be open to building new friendships. This protects the church from gravitating into cliques and spending our time only with those we feel comfortable around.

New Converts demand new levels of commitment and responsibility. As established Christians, we have to rise in our commitment to meet the demands of caring for and paying for an increasing membership. New converts means more support ministries, bigger facilities, and a larger hearted church.

We demonstrate our true commitment to the Great Commission by our willingness to pay for it

New Converts challenge our lifestyle as examples and ambassadors of our faith. We are the **example** to new Christians. The way we live and behave will be noted and taken as the standard of the church.

New Converts bring constant change to our environment. 'Conversion growth' brings healthy change like nothing else in the church.

New Converts generate joy and excitement, as each new Christian represents a miracle story, and with their story of salvation comes the joy of God, which they bring into the church.

New Converts enlarge our grace and tolerance. New Christians stumble and make mistakes. They break 'the rules' because they don't know 'the rules'. Every church must create an atmosphere of inclusion where new Christians are given room to grow and become established in their newfound faith.

New Converts are vital for Evangelism because every new Christian brings a new circle of influence into the Church, which presents opportunities for evangelism among their friends, family and associates. This is one of the keys we have discovered for growing the church.

CHAPTER TWO:

THE 'OIKOS' PRINCIPLE

While I was pioneering our church, I worked as an insurance agent and salesperson, and learnt an important principle that has proved to be vital in helping thousands of Christians become more effective witnesses in their world.

The principle is simply this: the most effective form of selling is through **personal referrals**.

There are several reasons for this. Firstly, a **satisfied customer** is the best marketer and qualifier of their friends, and secondly, **every person knows** between **thirty** and **seventy** people.

Personal Introduction to Christ is the Best!

Transferring this principle into evangelism is helpful. The best way to introduce people to Jesus Christ, therefore, is through personal referral and introduction.

Each Christian knows between thirty and seventy people in their world. They are already in contact with these people on a regular basis. They know them personally through the networks of involvements such as family, friends, associates, clients, clubs, recreation, neighbours, unions, associations and service and community groups.

In other words, every member of your church should be a 'satisfied customer' who is already networked with thirty to seventy people, and each of those friends and associates who becomes a Christian is networked with thirty to seventy people! The numbers become mind-blowing!

The Greek word "oikos" means "members of a household or family", which refers to a **circle of influence**, or a **network of people** related to one another through birth, career or common interest.

1. Common Kinship
2. Common Community
3. Common Career
4. Common Interest

This was the word used by the apostle Paul when he said to the Roman Prison Keeper, *"Believe on the Lord Jesus Christ, and you will be saved, you and your **household** ('oikos')."* *(Acts 16:31)*

The traditional eastern concept of 'household' is not familiar to the western mindset, but in eastern Bible times, it simply referred to a person's 'extended family' of connection and influence.

Paul understood that when the Prison Keeper became a Christian, he would immediately influence those in his 'oikos', that is, his family, friends, business associates, co-workers, and neighbours.

This is the kernel of Biblical witnessing, and the basic concept of 'Lifestyle Evangelism'.

Jesus chose his Apostles based on 'oikos'

The first chapter of John's Gospel records that after Andrew had believed in Christ, he went immediately and brought Peter, his brother, to hear Jesus (John 1:40-42).

It is also interesting to note that Andrew, Peter and Philip were all from Bethsaida and knew each other. Furthermore, the brothers James and John were acquaintances and business associates of all of these men as well.

Jesus understood the power of "oikos".

How to discover your 'oikos'

If the key to 'one-to-one evangelism' is through our normal network of relationships, who then are the people in my 'oikos'?

Do an inventory of your 'Oikos'

The first step is to do an inventory of your 'oikos', that is, write down everyone you know personally through common relationships and activities. Remember, as a guide, you should know between thirty and seventy people.

Examples to help you draw up your list are:

- Family
- Friends
- Neighbours
- Employers
- Employees
- Clients and Customers
- Business Owners and Staff
- Sports Group and Team members
- Service Organisation personnel
- Business Associates
- Health and Fitness Club colleagues
- Volunteer Organisation members
- Unions and professional organisation members

In the Appendix Section (1) you will find sample **'Oikos Inventory Sheets'** to help you.

"But I don't know anyone"

In just about every evangelism seminar and course that I have conducted over the past 45 years, I have discovered that many Christians have become isolated from non-Christians. Some have even admitted to not knowing any non-Christians on a personal basis!

The danger of 'enclaving'

One of the greatest hindrances to Christians being witnesses in their world, or 'oikos', is the process of 'enclaving', that is, the gradual withdrawal from and isolation of Christians from normal, social contact with the unchurched.

As a result, churches can become sub-cultures within their communities where Christians eventually lose their ability to relate significantly to the unchurched at all. In some church groups this is actually encouraged on 'holiness grounds', others subconsciously and indirectly, by providing everything for their members such as workplaces, sporting clubs, social activities and education where unchurched people are not included.

To effectively fulfill the command and example of our Lord Jesus Christ, churches must be more aware of the tendency to enclave, and boldly embrace evangelism as a lifestyle, rather than an occasional excursion into 'enemy territory'.

You are the Light of the World

Have you ever noticed that darkness never penetrates the light? At night, when a door is opened to the outside, a 'ray of darkness' doesn't enter the room; rather, a ray of light penetrates out into the darkness. Why is that? The answer is simple: light is more powerful than darkness!

As long as Christians believe that the darkness is greater than the light and is to be avoided at all costs, effective evangelism is not going to happen.

> *"You are the light of the world,*
> *a city that is set on a hill cannot be hidden."*
> *(Matthew 5:14)*

Our job is not to hide our light, to just be shared among the 'enlightened', our job is to let our light shine to those in darkness, the unenlightened, the lost.

> *"People do not light a lamp and put it under a basket*
> *but on a lampstand, and it gives light to all in the*
> *house. In the same way, let your light shine before*
> *people, so that they can see your good deeds and*
> *give honour to your Father in heaven."*
> *(Matthew 5:15-16)*

Some Candid Advice

If you are living a very narrow life and ask, "but what if I only know a few people and they're all Christians?" Something is very wrong with this picture.

My advice is, join a club or an association, start a hobby, meet some new people...anything! Get out and discover the real world.

How can we win non-Christians to Christ if we don't know any on a personal and social basis?

> *"How shall they hear without a preacher?"*
> *(Romans 10:20)*

God's plan has never been to take us out of the world, but rather, to send us into the world to be His channels of salvation and blessing. The issue is about the quality and strength of our faith, to be resistant and impenetrable from sin.

"I do not pray that You would take them out of the world, but that You would keep them from the evil."
(John 17:15)

Key questions to ask about the people in your 'oikos'

When thinking about the people in your 'oikos' and their readiness and willingness to genuinely listen to your story, it is important to understand how receptive and prepared they are. With this in mind, here are some key questions to ask:

1. What is the level or depth of your relationship with this person? "Have I built respect and trust so they will listen to me?"

2. What other Christians do they know well? "Who can I work with, or avoid (i.e. 'toxic Christians'), in order to lead my friend to Christ?"

3. How receptive are they? "Are my friends open to listen to my story and discuss the claims of Christ?"

4. How can this person's needs be met in our Church? Figure out what activity, special event, or small group they could fit into and relate to. For example, ladies groups, men's golf days, business or family seminars, social gatherings, dinner parties and youth and children's activities.

Cultivating Your 'Oikos'

The following check list will help you begin a journey to discover how strategically you are placed for God to start working miracles among your unsaved family, friends and associates:

1. **Use your inventory of your 'oikos' to start a 'Prayer List'**. Out of your thirty to seventy names, prayerfully select the six most receptive individuals and include them on your prayer list. Pray specifically for their salvation, and opportunities for you share your story with them. (See Appendix II 'Prayer List').

2. **Seek out social opportunities to develop your friendships** with the receptive non-Christians in your 'oikos'. I call this living in 'search mode'. To surf the net, a computer needs a search engine that is 'switched on'. The same is true in sharing your story. We need to be prayerfully in 'search mode', that is, alert, open and ready for the opportunities that arise among the family, friends, and associates in our 'oikos'.

3. **Don't watch the clock**. Be prepared for the long haul. Build relationships and the right to speak – this will take time.

Signs that your friends are ready

As we begin our journey of connecting with the people in our 'oikos', we will become more effective as we notice the signs that they are ready to engage in a deeper discussion about Christianity.

Some signs to watch for:

1. They enjoy being with you, their Christian friend.

2. Their religious background and experiences cease to be a hindrance for the Gospel.

3. They are curious about spiritual things and what happens in your church.

4. They take the initiative to include you in their social activities.

5. They are willing to participate in some church event, social function, special service, or guest speaker.

6. They become aware that the Gospel you share with them may contain answers to their own needs.

CHAPTER THREE:

BRIDGE BUILDING

The Latin word for "priest" is "pontifex", which literally means "bridge maker", or "builder" (Collins Dictionary). Jesus constantly built bridges into the lives of people from all walks of life. So much so, the Pharisees called Him "the friend of sinners".

Jesus built bridges with all kinds of people:

- Matthew, the tax collector
- The sinful woman
- The Pharisees
- Nicodemus, the ruler of the Jews
- The Samaritan woman
- The Royal official
- The criminal
- Jairus, the synagogue ruler

Jesus never condemned unsaved people, He showed them by His life and the power that worked within Him that living for God was the greatest experience.

The Bible also calls us "priests" (bridge makers). Our job is to build bridges into people's lives.

> *"You also, as living stones, are built up a spiritual house, a holy **priesthood**…" (1 Peter 2:5)*

We build bridges into the lives of our friends, neighbours and associates by making genuine friendships and by caring for and demonstrating God's love to them. 'Friendship-making' is the single most important component of effective witnessing because it takes us beyond mere 'friendliness' (being kind), to genuinely loving the person with God's love.

As we build bridges, we have found there are three pillars that need to be constructed that carry our bridge into the lives of people.

1. The Pillar of Credibility
2. The Pillar of Friendship
3. The Pillar of Answers

BRIDGE BUILDING PILLAR #1: CREDIBILITY

What is credibility?

Establishing credibility is very important to our witnessing. Credibility is simply the absence of contradictions from our lives that may hinder our message from being communicated. We lose credibility when things don't measure up. The more contradictions that occur, the harder it is to measure up.

The key is to relax and let your friends see you for who you really are…a genuine, 'normal' Christian friend. When we are credible, our unchurched friends can trust and believe that what we say is true!

CREDIBLE MEANS BELIEVABLE

'Lifestyle Evangelism' is a way of life, not a method. Church growth statistics show that most people come to church because a trusted friend brought them and introduced them to a Christian way of life that is credible.

WHY PEOPLE JOIN YOUR CHURCH From a Survey of over 8,000 people done by Dr. Win Arn of U.S.	
	%
Just came one Suday & stayed 'walk-ins'	5
The Pastor was main reason they joined	6
The Church programme was what they want	3
Through door to door visitation	1.999
Came in through Sunday School	4
Came through a Crusade or TV Programme	.0001
Brought by friends or relatives	80

BRIDGE BUILDING PILLAR #2: FRIENDSHIP

It's amazing how much the Bible teaches about making friends. Below are some insights from the Book of Proverbs on how to be a real friend:

1. We have to learn how to be a loyal friend in times of trouble. (Proverbs 17:17)
2. Keep secrets to yourself. (Proverbs 11:13)
3. Don't keep bringing up past mistakes. (Proverbs 17:9)
4. Keep all friendships open, that is, include other people in your life - don't be a 'one friend person'. (Proverbs 25:17)
5. Friendships are built on sacrificial love. All relationships require giving to make them work. (John 15:13)
6. True friends are open to shared disapproval and advice. (Proverbs 27:6)

How does 'Friendship Evangelism' work?

The first thing about friendship evangelism is that we have to contact people socially. It's helpful to adopt the Biblical view of evangelism as fishing and ask the question, "Where are the fish?" Are they in the bath? No, they're in the rivers and the seas! Fishing is experienced when you get out among the fish – this fact is unavoidable!

Where are our unchurched friends? They're at home, work, at the beach, in cafes, sporting and fitness activities, pubs and at the football. We cannot contact non-Christians at church – they don't come to church. We must get out among our non-Christian friends and be genuine friends to them.

The McCrindle research group ("Faith and Belief in Australia" 2016) reveals that 52% of Australians identify as Christians. 1 in 4 Australians (24%) are warm towards Christianity and

1 in 8 (12%) are neutral towards Christianity. Research indicates that 36% of Australians (8.64 million) are not against Christianity. Similar surveys in other western countries reveal the same statistics.

USA Stats (Barna Research 2016)

*   31% of Americans are church attenders
*   73% say they are Christian
*   20% claim no faith at all (including agnostics and atheists)

CANADA Stats (MacLean Research 2016)

*   23% of Canadians are church attenders
*   73% believe in a God or higher power

UNITED KINGDOM (Faith Survey 2016)

*   5% of British are church attenders
*   59.5% say they are Christian
*   28% believe in a God or higher power

SINGAPORE (Strait Times, March 2016)

% Christian
* 2010 18.3%
* 2015 18.8%

% No Religion
* 15-34yrs 45%
* 35-44yrs 19.4%
= Total 64.4%

If we fail to connect with our non-Christian friends, relatives and associates in their world, where they are at, God has no other channel through which to reach them because God has ordained us to be His channel…WE'RE IT!

"All power is given unto me in heaven and in earth.
You go therefore, *and teach all nations, baptizing*
them in the name of the Father, and of the Son, and of
the Holy Spirit." (Matthew 28:18-19)

We have to garner interest by learning how to be a 'baiter of hooks'. The key to any person's heart is what they have a passion for; whether that be sports, music, art, travel, hobbies and interests. We have to listen, observe and research their areas of interest, and participate in their hobbies and interests in order to relate effectively with them. Some Christians may object at this point and exclaim, "But what if my unchurched friends are a bad influence?" The answer is: choose and involve yourself in activities that aren't sinful. There are plenty of 'sin free' opportunities.

Here's what I've discovered: If you involve yourself in those things that interest and inspire you, you will naturally meet people who have a passion for the same things and you will find it easier to build great friendships.

We have to be patient and be committed for the long haul. There is no need to 'rush in' and arouse distrust and suspicion instead of genuine interest.

One of the most important things we have to learn is how to cultivate and encourage people, not condemn them. It's easy to condemn. Think about the type of person you were before becoming a Christian.

Learn to show genuine interest in people and encourage positive traits, habits and beliefs. For example, your friend discloses, "I've started going to Meditation, I find it relaxing." To which you could reply, "Meditation is of the devil!" (followed by an argument), or, "You're obviously interested in spiritual things, aren't you?" (followed by a discussion on 'spirituality').

When relating to our unchurched friends it's easy to get involved in 'side tracks'. For example, my friends have often commented, "I could never go to church because you're against smoking and drinking etc.". These issues are 'side tracks' and not relevant to a person being loved by God or receiving salvation. God doesn't make an issue of these things, so why should we? An encounter with God and the process of discipleship will settle all these issues for your friend.

Above all things, our clear objective is to introduce people to Jesus Christ. If we truly live for Jesus Christ our unsaved friends will see His life in us and will give rise to questions being asked by them.

"But sanctify the Lord God in your hearts: and be ready always to give an answer to every man that asks you a reason of the hope that is in you with meekness and fear." (1 Peter 3:15)

Some practical advice

1. The unchurched will ask you what's different about you, be ready to give an answer.

2. Get involved with unchurched associations and clubs, not just Christian ones.

3. Capitalise on holidays, festivals and celebrations. Special occasions make it easier to invite people.

4. Be available and present in times of crisis and need.

5. Look for the appropriate 'handle', that is, something in your Church that will interest them. For example, a guest speaker, special service, or a special event.

BRIDGE BUILDING PILLAR #3: ANSWERS TO QUESTIONS

" ...always be prepared to give an answer (or defense) to everyone who asks you to give a reason for the hope that you have..." (1 Peter 3:15)

"The heart of the righteous studies how to answer..." (Proverbs 15:28)

Answering the heartfelt questions, concerns and objections of our unchurched friends is very important. The Bible teaches us to be prepared to answer.

There are seven basic questions that are commonly asked by the unchurched:

Q1: "WILL THE PERSON WHO HAS NEVER HEARD OF JESUS CHRIST BE CONDEMNED?"

In other words, what about people who do not have the Bible? What about those who have never heard the Gospel? Will God be fair? Will He treat them the same as us?

It is important to explain that God is totally just and fair. He shows no partiality. All men will give an account to God on the basis of God's justice, not our own. We will all get a fair trial!

In the book of Romans, chapters two and three, the Word of God clearly teaches that those who have the Law will be judged by the Law (Romans 2:12), and those who do not have the Law will be judged without the law, that is, by their conscience and intelligence.

God will judge all people by what they see and know about God in creation (Romans 1:19-20), and by their own conscience and intelligence (Romans 2:15).

Q2: "IS JESUS THE ONLY WAY TO GOD?"

The key issue in this question is one of truth. Jesus is either wrong (isn't the only way to God), or right (is the only way to God).

Which is true? Universalism teaches one God and many ways to God, whereas the Scriptures teach there is only one way to God through the Lord Jesus Christ.

> *"Neither is there salvation in any other: for there is none other name under Heaven given among men, whereby we must be saved." (Acts 4:12)*

A study of world religions explains this by making informed comparisons between Christ and other religious leaders and their claims.

All religions can be classified into the following three groups:

1. No God
2. One God
3. God Everywhere

Another way of looking at things is that there are basically two groups of religions in the world:

1. Those similar to Christianity
2. Those with few or no similarities

Islam, for example, is similar to Christianity in some respects. For example, doctrinal agreements – one God, a created universe etc. but in terms of the nature of God, the nature of man, Jesus Christ and sin, it is totally different.

On the other hand, other religions like Buddhism are so different to Christianity because they hold a pantheistic world-view, which believes that God and the material world are one and the same. Everyone and everything in the material world is part of the Divine.

The conclusion: Christianity stands out by itself and is different.

A helpful way is to try and look from God's viewpoint and imagine you are God. On planet earth there are over seven billion people and you want them to find you.

Wouldn't it be absurd for you to offer a million different ways for people to find you? Why throw confusion in? Wouldn't it be logical to give one way to show the way? Unless you didn't really want people to find you!

Only one person ever claimed to know the way to God, the Lord Jesus Christ, for He declared, *"I am the way, the truth and the life." (John 14:6)*

Q3: "HOW CAN MIRACLES BE POSSIBLE?"

The key issues in this question are: a. Does God exist? And, if so, b. Does God perform miracles?

It is important to understand from the outset that we can't prove **conclusively** that God does exist. If honest, the atheist must admit that he/she doesn't know everything and, therefore, can't prove conclusively that God doesn't exist.

But I believe we can prove **sufficiently** that God does exist.

Why do people ask this question "Does God really exist?"

To accept that God does exist we must logically accept that God is able to perform miracles, otherwise He is not God! Therefore, the key is not to argue whether miracles are true or not, but rather to talk about the existence of God.

If God exists, then miracles happen.

Another related question being asked here is; "If the Bible is wrong and full of errors, does God exist?"

Here's the thing: After 2000 years, no one is going to come up with a new question or proof against the Bible! The Bible has been banned, burnt, and debated by experts, but it is still the No.1 best seller in the world!

When confronted with this question I ask, "have you read the Bible?" In most cases I receive the same answer, "No". To which I reply, "Then how do you know for sure that the Bible is full of errors?"

To aid discussion, it is often helpful to define the word 'error' – is there an error because the Bible…

- contradicts what you or others believe?
- contradicts other Scriptures?

Q5: "AREN'T CHRISTIAN EXPERIENCES PSYCHOLOGICAL?"

This question undermines a person's Christian experience as merely psychological and not real, and therefore raises the question of, "Does God exist?"

The fact still remains; people wouldn't change from other beliefs and lifestyles purely on a psychological basis - it is unsustainable.

The very question tends to belittle a Christian experience on one hand, and yet on the other hand cannot answer the fact that more people are becoming Christians today than in any other time in history.

It is important to share your personal, life-changing experience and a miracle you know has personally happened to you – your testimony.

Also, discussing man's nature can help. We are comprised of a body, soul and spirit.

- Body - physical
- Soul - intellect and personality
- Spiritual - conscience and spiritual awareness

It is important to point out that just because we can't see or show spiritual reality, doesn't mean it isn't real or doesn't exist. We have spiritual capacities so we can worship God. Not everything in this world can be explained or examined by scientific or physical means.

Another important thing to discuss is the human problem of guilt. When we sin we feel guilty. This is the real, unseen faculty of human conscience.

Q6: "WON'T A GOOD MORAL LIFE GET ME TO HEAVEN?"

The case being proposed by this question is; "Isn't man basically good?" The conclusion being that we don't need God.

A human, self-sufficient position, however, is a fallacy. A totally self-sufficient person must be an absolute, complete being, who needs no one or nothing.

There are two unsustainable arguments in this position:

- man isn't really evil or commits evil
- man's intellect and will is sufficiently superior

The person asking this question is showing a belief in an incorrect concept of God. It shows no understanding about the eternity and finality of God.

The major problem with this idea is that all human beings

have the power to live by the 'Golden Rule', however, living by the rule means the rule becomes the judge. The self-sufficiency of man is a fallacy. If not, why do we live in a world tainted and complicated by human errors and imperfections?

We all need to talk about and deal with repentance. God's major issue with us is that we refuse to accept Him, and continue to present ourselves as something we're not – perfect.

Q7: "WHY DO THE INNOCENT SUFFER?"

The real question being asked here is; "Is God a loving and just God? Is He the origin of all that befalls us – good and evil alike?

There are two kinds of people who ask this type of question:

1. People asking out of a genuine desire to know – they genuinely want to know and ask the following:

    a. Is God a loving, just God?

    b. What is God's motive towards mankind?

    c. If God could prevent the suffering of the innocent, why doesn't He do so, isn't He powerful enough?

When discussing this issue, the common misconceptions are:

- God's love and justice are incompatible
- God is the origin of all that befalls us – 'God made it happen.'

The Bible clearly teaches us that God is not the origin of everything that befalls us! Chance happens to us (Ecclesiastes 9:11), the devil does things to us (1John 3:8) and we cause a lot of problems through our own disobedience and lack of wisdom (James 4:1-3)!

2. They have a grief that is a known experience.

It is helpful to show your friend that everything that happens doesn't come from God. God has given humans a free will – we choose whether to lie, fight or steal, both individually and as nations.

"Where do wars and fightings come from among you? Don't they come from your lusts that war in your members? You lust, and have not: you kill, and desire to have, and cannot obtain: you fight and war, yet you have not, because you ask not. You ask, and receive not, because you ask amiss, that you may consume it upon your lusts." (James 4:1)

Man was created under the protection of God but chose to be independent of Him. Therefore, all humanity and the environment was exposed to evil. God grieves over this constantly and desires man to be saved from this evil.

God also grieves daily over the innocent suffering. When each soul who repents is saved, there is rejoicing in heaven (Luke 16:10). God is innocent yet He suffers every day. God grieved over Jesus, who suffered for us.

If God doesn't care, why are most of the humanitarian aid organisations in the world Christian? Could this be the appeal of God through Christians to do something about those suffering in the world?

KEYS TO BRIDGE BUILDING

When it comes to lifestyle evangelism, we must first build the 'bridge of love' so we can drive the 'train of truth' across.

The most import starting point is to avoid "Bible Bashing" and Verse Quoting. Rule number one in witnessing by lifestyle to our friends and associates is to leave our Bibles at home and live Christ in their world (we don't just preach Christ verbally!)

It is also vital that we change our terminology and avoid 'speaking in a foreign language' aka 'Christianese', which usually centers on spiritual and hidden significant meanings that the unchurched (even many Christians) don't understand. We must learn the art of communicating with our friends in a way that they understand.

Of course, lifestyle evangelism won't happen without a change in our lifestyle. We will have to adjust our social calendars and involve our unchurched friends and colleagues in our lives by inviting and including them in our social activities.

One thing we have to do as Christians is learn to accept non-Christian behaviour as 'normal', for them. We must never forget how we used to live before we met Christ!

When we are shocked at non-Christian behaviour, we will be unable to build a relationship. We must not expect the unchurched to live as Christians – it is not going to happen until they are changed by the power of God!

CHAPTER FOUR:

CONVERSATIONAL WITNESSING

The art of conversational communication is a skill that is essential to be effective in sharing our faith and can be developed with practice. Can you imagine Philip the evangelist arguing or preaching *at* the Ethiopian diplomat instead of engaging in effective conversation *with* him? The results could have been very different!

Conversational witnessing is effective because it is an approach that:

1. Knows how to convert Biblical facts, or concepts, into 'people benefits'
2. Knows how to create the right climate for communication
3. Knows how to relate by asking the right questions
4. Knows how to eliminate contradictions and offences

Understanding Conversation

Human communication is made up of about 10% words spoken, 25% tone of voice and 65% body language, so it is important to develop the skills of communication to be effective as a witness of Christ.

We do this first of all by showing genuine interest in the person. Be a 'giver' not a 'getter'. Remember, conversation is the reciprocal sharing of ideas, feelings and thoughts.

It is important to be sensitive to what people are saying. We do this through body language, concentrating on listening, and asking questions such as why, what and when?

In conversation, we must always resist distractions and the temptation to argue. It is therefore important to maintain eye contact and learn to concentrate on the person and their needs.

One of the biggest mistakes in conversation is to interject. Allow the other person to finish their statements. Also, it's wise to avoid taking up minor points, or unimportant opinions. Failure to do this will result in debate and strife, instead of positive conversation. This is how we create the right environment for communication.

We all need to put some thought into our conversation, to learn how to think ahead and guide the conversation around to Christ. We can achieve this by asking questions such as, "Suppose someone asked you, 'what is a Christian?' What would you say a Christian is?" and agreeing and confirming the other person's comments, like, "I can see that you're interested in spiritual things."

Our strategy in witnessing is to keep our conversation at the level of the heart. We achieve this by focusing on our story and experiences, answers to their questions and explaining how this all relates to what the Word of God has to say on the matter.

CHAPTER FIVE:

TELL YOUR STORY

"Be READY ALWAYS to give an ANSWER to every man that asks you a REASON of the hope that is in you with meekness and fear."

(1 Peter 3:15)

There will come a time when your friends will want to know your story. This is an undeniable fact for those who truly live Christ among their unchurched friends.

At the right time, it is essential that you present the Gospel in a clear, logical and compelling manner. This will only happen when we are "ready", that is, prepared to give an answer.

The Apostle Paul's encounter in Acts chapter 25 with King Agrippa sets out several key principles regarding presenting the Gospel that are helpful to us.

The first thing that Paul did was to establish his right to be heard. He appealed to Caesar (Acts 25:21) and used his citizenship and right to be heard as a Roman. This meant he understood the social customs and manners and was therefore respectful of them before his hearers.

EARNING THE RIGHT TO BE HEARD IS ABOUT BECOMING AN AUTHENTIC VOICE IN THE EARS OF YOUR HEARERS

Secondly, Paul spoke with a respectful and happy disposition. In other words, he was positive and confident.

> *"I think myself happy, King Agrippa, because today*
> *I shall answer for myself before you concerning*
> *all things of which I am accused by the Jews."*
> *(Acts 26:2)*

Thirdly, Paul acknowledged King Agrippa's expertise in the subject. He included him in the discussion.

> *"Especially because I know you to be expert in all*
> *the customs and questions which are among the*
> *Jews: wherefore I beseech you to hear me patiently."*
> *(Acts 26:3)*

The 'BC, RC & LC' Format

Fourthly, and very importantly, Paul presented his story in a logical manner. He did this by dividing his story into three parts: 'BC' (before Christ), 'RC' (receiving Christ) and 'LC' (living Christ).

- **"Before Christ"** – Paul clearly summarised his life as a non-christian as being a committed opponent of the faith.

- **"Receiving Christ"** – Paul spent time sharing how he met Christ on the road to Damascus, what happened to him and how this experience dramatically changed his life forever.

- **"Living Christ"** – Paul then shared how he now lived by being obedient to God and the vision, and presented the Gospel in a nutshell to him.

In our church small groups, we have spent time helping our members write out and rehearse their story using the 'BC, RC and LC' format so when they have the opportunity, they will be ready and confident to present their testimony in a logical and compelling way.

"A PREPARED DEMONSTRATION (TESTIMONY) MEANS PERSONALISED"
Jeffrey Gitomer

The '30-3-30 Principle'

This is where the '30-3-30 Principle' comes into effect.

We must be aware of the setting and the time opportunity to be effective witnesses. '30' equals 30 seconds, '3' equals 3 minutes and '30' equals 30 minutes. We need prepared responses for the three different 'time opportunities' that will be presented to us.

Write out your story in the three time formats ('30-3-30') so you will be able to respond with confidence.

For example, when a friend asks us why we go to church, that is often just a '30 second moment', not a '30 minute moment'.

30 Second Sample Response

Unchurched friend: "Is it true that you go to church?"

Me: "Yes, before becoming a Christian, I was struggling with so many things and felt really unfulfilled, but then I met Jesus and that changed for me. I'd love to catch up over coffee sometime and chat more about it if you like. Can you pass me the sugar?"

Fifthly, Paul confidently refuted the hearer's objections when Festus explained, *"Paul, you are beside yourself! Much learning is driving you mad."* (Acts 26:24)

Paul maintained his poise and purpose and respectfully replied. *"I am not mad most noble Festus, but speak the words of truth and reason"*. (Acts 26:25)

Sixthly, Paul personalized the claims of the Gospel to his hearers by drawing Agrippa personally into his presentation by commending him. *"The King knows these things; for I am convinced that none of these things escapes his attention."*

Finally, Paul followed with a direct personal question to King Agrippa; *"King Agrippa, do you believe the prophets? I know that you do believe"*, and so left King Agrippa 'almost persuaded' to become a Christian.

Our goal in presenting the Gospel should always be to bring

people closer to 'almost persuaded'. Our non-Christian friends can be considered to be on a 'minus scale' below zero, depending on their attitude, experience and knowledge of Christ.

EVERY STORY IS A MIRACLE
EVERY MIRACLE IS A NEW LIFE
EVERY NEW LIFE IS A STORY
TELL YOUR STORY

MOVING PEOPLE TOWARDS RECEPTIVITY

In Lifestyle Evangelism, the key is to help move our friends along the line of receptivity in an encouraging and patient way. Remember, you are not in a hurry! Identifying where your unchurched friend might be in terms of receptivity is very helpful.

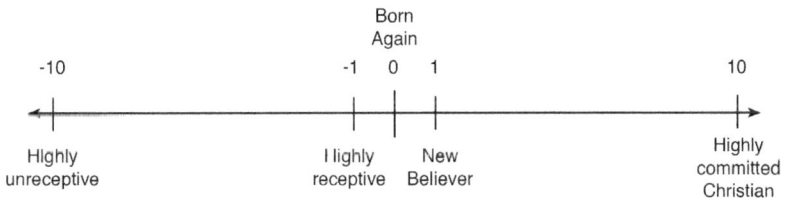

Born Again

-10   -1 0 1   10

Highly
unreceptive   Highly
receptive   New
Believer   Highly
committed
Christian

CHAPTER SIX:

THE POWER OF ACTS OF KINDNESS

"Do you not know that God's kindness leads you to repentance?"

(Romans 2:15)

My wife bought a pair of quality, fashion sunglasses that she loved.

Unfortunately, some screws fell out so I offered to get them fixed. I took them to several stores, all of which didn't repair or didn't have the screws! I tried a sunglasses kiosk stand on the way out of the shopping center thinking; of course they will charge me.

When I returned to pick up the glasses and pay, the assistant said, "Sir, there is no charge and I also gave them a thorough clean, and included some cleaning fluid and a cleaning cloth for your wife." I responded, "Are you sure?" "Sir, I'm pleased that I was able to help you." She replied with a smile. **WOW!** That's real service and of course, I've recommended her to several of my friends!

Jesus had the same approach.

When invited to a wedding of a family friend, the hosts ran out of wine. Jesus went above what was expected and not only performed a miracle of turning water into wine; he provided the highest quality wine... *"You have kept the best wine until the end."* (John 2:10)

Acts of kindness and generosity stand out and cause people to say "WOW!" The reason? We have made their day, we have added value to them as a human being and created a memorable moment for them that they will never forget!

Acts of kindness open up opportunities and create connections and friendships with people.

When was the last time somebody said "WOW!" to you about something you did for them or for someone else? Have you ever had an act of kindness done to you where you exclaimed, "WOW"? If you have, you'll never forget it!

But here's the reality about acts of kindness; they don't happen very often. That's why when they do happen, we all think and say, "WOW"!

In order to be 'extra-ordinary' in this life, practice acts of kindness regularly and you will stand out, especially among your unchurched friends and colleagues.

So what do acts of kindness look like? The simple answer is this: whatever is appropriate, will add value and make the moment memorable for your friend or colleague.

Acts of kindness can include; staying behind at work to help finish a project deadline, bringing coffee, writing a note of appreciation, visiting a friend or colleague in hospital, taking cooked meals to a sick friend, buying a gift for a new baby, sending flowers or a card for a bereavement… the list is never ending!

Opportunities for acts of kindness occur every day. All we need to do is be prepared, and look and respond with a heart of love and generosity.

CHAPTER SEVEN:

"COOK IT AND THEY WILL COME"

"Don't forget to show hospitality to strangers, for in doing so, some have entertained angels without knowing it."

(Hebrews 13:2)

Being generous with hospitality is the easiest way to make friends and open the hearts of people.

Hospitality is common to the human experience for all generations, races, ages and stages. The 'table of hospitality' creates a natural setting for friendship connection to happen around a meal or a drink together. Hospitality creates an atmosphere of inclusion.

The Table in Paradise

The remarkable thing about Jesus is that He revolved so much of His ministry and teaching around the meal table. His first miracle was turning the water into wine for a friend's wedding feast. That's why the Pharisees called Him *"a glutton and winebibber"* (Matthew 11:19).

Jesus promised his disciples that after He had ascended into Heaven, there would await the keeping of a meal of celebration in Heaven for all the faithful. God has opened His heart and Heavenly home to all who would accept His invitation.

> *"But I tell you that I will not drink of this fruit of the vine from now on, until that day when I drink it anew with you in my Father's Kingdom." (Matthew 26:29)*

The apostle Paul includes hospitality as a qualification of leadership (1Timothy 3:2). Why is this? Because a hospitable person is a generous person, an including person, a serving person and a selfless person, true qualities of a leader.

This is the direct opposite of the Pharisees who "eat by themselves". In other words, outsiders are not welcome! Pharisees do not possess a serving and hospitable spirit, but "love the best (prominent) seats" at feasts.

The example of the inhospitable Simon the Pharisee is recorded in Luke's Gospel (Luke 7:44-46). Simon had invited Jesus to his house so he could discuss and debate technical points of the Law. However, Jesus censored Simon in front of the "sinful woman", who was not invited, because he had broken every rule of eastern hospitality: "You gave me no water to wash my feet, neither did you greet me and welcome into your home" and "you gave me no oil for my head".

Hospitality was central in the life and ministry of Jesus. John's Gospel reveals this by beginning with a wedding party (John 2) and ending with a breakfast BBQ on the beach (John 21).

Natural, organic evangelism

In Acts 2 we read that the early church lived, worked and ministered around the table of hospitality:

"They devoted themselves daily to meeting together in the temple complex corporate and broke their bread from House to House. They ate their food with gladness and simplicity of heart..." (Acts 2:46 NET)

The key ideas of this kind of hospitality are togetherness, food, gladness (joy, laughter and fun) and simplicity. This is the environment in which evangelism can happen naturally, organically and effectively.

"Praising God and having favour with all the people. And everyday the Lord added to the church those who were being saved."

"COOK IT AND THEY WILL COME"

CHAPTER EIGHT:

"THE BIG ASK"

I watched many great movies with my kids over the years and one of my favorite scenes is from the movie "Labyrinth", where the fox, Didymus, who had sworn on his life to protect a bridge, exclaimed to the heroes, "No one shall pass this way without my permission!" To which the heroine, Sarah, asked after much fighting and misunderstanding occurred, "Well, may we have your permission?" To which Didymus replied, even surprising himself, "Yes!" No one had ever asked for his permission!

The moral of the story: often our unchurched friends have not responded to Christ yet simply because no one has actually asked them! I call this 'The Big Ask'.

So how do we open up a discussion on anything, with anyone? How do we ask in such a way that we get a positive response?

We have to ask the right questions!

Unchurched Survey (Australian NCLS)

The unchurched are surveyed by the National Church Life Survey (NCLS) every five years in Australia and the results are very interesting (my experience shows me that this is the same across the world).

1. "Have you ever been invited to church?"
   90% = "NO"

2. "Would you go to church if you were invited?"
   70% = "YES"

"The Big Ask"

This is encouraging because most of our unchurched friends would say yes to our invitation… THE BIG ASK.

The right questions will lead you to information and agreement...ENGAGEMENT

Have you ever encountered a sales assistant who has no idea how to engage you in a 'buying discussion'?

The conversation usually goes like this:

Sales assistant: "Can I help you?"
You: "No thanks"
Sales Assistant: "No worries let me know if you need me."
You: Leave the store.

Why does this happen so frequently? Because sales assistants so often ask the wrong questions!

How different things turn out when the conversation goes something like this:

Sales Assistant: "Hi, my name is John (smiling and friendly), are you looking for (because you're thumbing through the shirt rack) a shirt for business or a holiday?"
You: "Ah… business."
Sales Assistant: "And does your work involve travel, or are you based mainly here?"
You: "I travel quite a bit."
Sales Assistant: "Great! In that case, I don't think these shirts will be exactly what you're looking for. Over here (leading you to another rack) are some shirts better suited to your needs because they are made from a more durable and breathable fabric that is better for travel. I'm actually wearing one today. Do you have to wear casual, or more formal attire for work?"
You: "Both".
Sales Assistant: "Then may I suggest these options for you? The black and white shirts would be ideal for a more formal look… is there one you prefer?"

You: "I like both, actually."
Sales Assistant: "Would you like to buy one, or both today?"
You: "Both!"

Do you get the idea?

Even though this is a sales illustration, the application is huge for us in witnessing!

For example, have you ever extended an invitation to a friend or colleague to come to an event at church? Maybe it went like this:

You: "Would you like to come to our Christmas Show at church?"
Friend: "No thanks"
You: "Ok."
Friend: Never comes.

Why does this happen so frequently? Because we often ask the wrong questions!

How differently things can turn out when the conversation goes something like this:

You: "Hey John, I managed to secure these tickets with reserved seating for us at my church's Christmas show on Christmas Eve. There will be dinner afterwards in the café too…how about I pick you up at 5:30pm?"
Friend: "Ah… Ok."
You: "What drink would you like with your dinner so I can preorder?"
Friend: "Oh, thanks! What drinks do they have?"
You: "Coffee to order, chocolate, tea and a selection of cold drinks."
Friend: "Hot chocolate."
You: "Done. Pick you up at 5:30pm Christmas Eve."

Friend: Comes to Christmas Show and loves it!

The questions we ask are so important. We need to ask ourselves these questions:

Do you want to get others to think?

...All you have to do is ask the right questions

Do you want to get others to act?

...All you have to do is ask the right questions

Do you want to get others to respond?

...All you have to do is ask the right questions

Do you want to get others to receive?

...All you have to do is ask the right questions

Here are some ideas about the 'right kind' of questions:

- Ask questions that **avoid "Yes" and "No" answers**
- Ask questions that make people **evaluate new information**
- Ask questions that **qualify needs**
- Ask questions that **remove objections**
- Ask questions that make people **think before giving a response**
- Ask questions that create a **'buying atmosphere'** as opposed to a **'selling atmosphere'**
- **Ask positive questions that assume a positive answer!**

ASK WRONG QUESTIONS, GET WRONG ANSWERS

Have you ever noticed that this is not a new idea?

God has always asked questions:

1. "Where are you?" (Genesis 3:9)
2. "Who told you you were naked?" (Genesis 3:11)
3. "Have you eaten from the tree of which I commanded you not to eat?" (Genesis 3:11)
4. "What is this you have done?" (Genesis 4:10)
5. "Why are you angry? And why has your countenance fallen?" (Genesis 4:6)
6. "If you do well, will you not be accepted?" (Genesis 4:7)
7. "Where is Abel your brother?" (Genesis 4:9)
8. "What are you doing here, Elijah?" (1Kings 19:9)
9. "Will a man rob God?" (Malachi 3:8)
10. "But who do you say that I am?" (Matthew 16:15)
11. "Whose is this image and superscription?" (Matthew 22:20)
12. "What is written in the law? What is your reading of it?" (Luke 10:26)
13. "So which of these three do you think was neighbor to him who fell among thieves?" (Luke 10:36)
14. "If a son asks for bread from any father among you, will he give him a stone? Or if he asks for a fish, will he give him a serpent instead of a fish? Or if he asks for an egg, will he offer him a scorpion?" (Luke 11:11-12)

The questioning approach by Philip the Evangelist (Acts 8:29-35)

The account of Philip the evangelist's discussion with the Ethiopian diplomat illustrates the importance of asking questions to open the heart of a receptive person.

Philip moved very logically and clearly by the way he positioned himself and by the questions he asked:

1. Philip obeyed the prompting of the Holy Spirit

*"Then the Spirit said unto Philip, Go near, and **join yourself** to this chariot."*

2. Philip opened the conversation with a question

*"And Philip ran to him, and heard him read the prophet Esaias, and said, **Do you understand what you are reading?**"*

3. The Diplomat responded with his desire to learn

*"And he said, **How can I, except some man should guide me?** And he **desired** Philip that he would come up and **sit with him**."*

"The place of the scripture which he read was this, He was led as a sheep to the slaughter; and like a lamb dumb before his shearer, so opened he not his mouth: In his humiliation his judgment was taken away: and who shall declare his generation? for his life is taken from the earth."

4. Philip waited for the Diplomat to ask his question

"And the eunuch answered Philip, and said, I pray you, of whom does the prophet speak? Of himself, or of some other man?"

5. Philip began at the place where he found the Diplomat

*"Then Philip opened his mouth, and **began at the same scripture**, and **preached unto him Jesus**."*

WHAT QUESTIONS COULD YOU ASK YOUR FRIEND THAT COULD OPEN UP THEIR LIFE TO A WHOLE NEW DESTINY IN CHRIST?

Preparation to ask the Right Questions

The preparation and thought we put into our discussion and questions with our friends is vital. It's no good making up your answer on the spot or fishing through your mind to find an answer!

"The heart of the righteous studies to answer."
(Proverbs 15:28)

It's a good idea to start by writing out a list of the questions that you think will open up discussion with your friend.

Also, develop a list of as many objections that you would need to answer for your friend to be receptive to accepting Christ and find answers for them.

CHAPTER NINE:

EVANGELISM AND YOUR CHURCH

"And the Lord ADDED TO THE CHURCH daily those who were being saved."

(Acts 2:42)

Evangelism without connection to a local church family is a fruitless activity. It may be a 'Christian activity', but it is not what God has intended.

Let me explain.

Leading a friend to Christ but not joining them to a local church family is the same as a young couple giving birth to a child and leaving the child at the hospital. "Where is your child?" someone might ask. "We don't know, I guess the doctors and nurses are looking after it." We would condemn such unthinkable and irresponsible actions by parents, and rightly so, because everyone knows it takes a family environment to raise healthy children.

The same is true in God's family. It takes a local church family environment to raise and grow healthy Christians.

The Apostle Paul's revelation of the local church family as outlined in his letter to the Ephesians is central to our understanding and practice of the local church today.

*"Of whom the whole **family** in **heaven** and **earth** is named." (Ephesians 3:15)*

*"Now therefore ye are no more strangers and foreigners, but fellow citizens with the saints, and of the **household of God**; And are built upon the foundation of the apostles and prophets, Jesus Christ himself being the chief corner stone; In whom all the building fitly framed together grows unto an holy temple in the Lord: In whom you also are built together for an habitation of God through the Spirit." (Ephesians 2:19)*

According to the apostle Paul's teaching, we are no longer "foreigners and strangers" (or 'orphans'), but are made children of God through the 'New Birth' and members of "the household ('family') of God". Notice how he goes on to describe how God has "fitted us together" (WEB Translation), or "joined us together" (NET Translation), into His family. It is in this context of the community and family of faith that we grow and progress in our faith in Christ.

"God sets the solitary in families: he brings out those who are bound with chains: but the rebellious dwell in a dry land." (Psalm 68:6)

When a child is born, they are born automatically into a family. The same thing happens when a new Christian is born again, they are born automatically into their church family.

Here are some of the key things that happen to the new born child of God when they are joined to their local church family:

- Obtainment of spiritual DNA of local church family – the spirit of faith, hope and love.

- Given the Church family name.

- Provided with Church family rights of love, support, participation and protection – followed up, nurtured and protected by leaders and members.

- Established as a 'legal heir' of their Church family inheritance and heritage – shares in the spiritual mission and ministry of their Church family.

When we understand that effective evangelism is from, through and to the local church family, the results of our witnessing will dramatically improve. This is because our witnessing will no longer be limited to just seeking a decision to accept Christ 'personally', but rather an invitation to accept the call of God to live a new life for Christ 'corporately' in and through the community of faith, the local church.

*"Then **they** that gladly received his word were baptized: and the same day there were **added unto them** about three thousand souls. And **they** continued steadfastly in the apostles' doctrine and fellowship, and in breaking of bread, and in prayers."*
(Acts 2:41-42)

*"And **they**, continuing daily with one accord in the temple, and breaking bread from house to house, did eat their food with gladness and singleness of heart, Praising God, and having favour with all the people. And the Lord **added to the church** daily those who were being saved." (Acts 2:46-47)*

The local church is a prime connector of people to God. By this we are not saying that people can't find God personally apart from direct contact with a Church, or even a Christian, however, we do believe they will need to be part of a Church family to make their Christian life work the way God intended it to work.

Therefore, building and focusing the local Church around the attraction of the unchurched (evangelism) and the establishing of New Christians (discipleship) is the core mission of the Church.

"All power is given unto me in heaven and in earth. Go therefore, and teach all nations, baptising them in the name of the Father, and of the Son, and of the Holy Spirit: Teaching them to observe all things I have commanded you: and, lo, I am with you always, even unto the end of the world. Amen."
(Matthew 28:18-20)

How can churches become more effective in fulfilling this command of Jesus?

The answer is simple: by focusing all ministry, resources and efforts in the local church towards the attracting, winning and assimilating of the unchurched into the Church family.

"A CHURCH FOR THE UNCHURCHED"

We are called by God to create a church environment and culture that welcomes the unchurched, just like our Lord Jesus Christ:

> *"I came not to call the righteous, but sinners to repentance." (Luke 5:32)*

When every pastor, leader and member of our churches recognises that "our church doesn't exist for me, our church exists for the unchurched, the lost, those who haven't discovered Jesus yet", we will experience effective evangelism like we've never seen before!

AS LONG AS ONE PERSON IN OUR COMMUNITY DOESN'T KNOW THE LORD, WE'RE OPEN FOR BUSINESS!

Here's the bottom line: When we build the church through evangelism we are doing exactly what Christ does… His work!

To create 'Unchurched Biased Churches' we are not proposing mobilising Christians into programs and traditional forms of outreach, as these have been found to be largely ineffective in building the local church. Rather, we are proposing the training and mobilizing of Christians by the church into the marketplace to live Christ and share their faith with their friends, family and colleagues on a daily basis… 'lifestyle evangelism'.

Here is a list of some ideas and ways every local Church can create an 'unchurched bias':

1. Rewrite your Church Vision/Purpose Statement with, 'Souls' at the top ("Reach Unchurched People")!

2. Cast the vision to win souls at every opportunity. We have given weekly updates to the church on how many people "said yes to Jesus". This generates so much excitement and enthusiasm for evangelism.

3. Include the prayer for the unsaved as the top need in every church prayer meeting.

4. Gear all services and events towards the unchurched – music, clothing, terminology, speakers, topics and provide a variety of styles of services and events.

5. Provide visitor car parks – the best and most accessible to services. These need to be clearly signed and located.

6. Provide benefits for visitors – complimentary drinks and information packs on the church with reserved seating in the café and events, making their attendance an occasion to remember.

7. Require all small groups to conduct 'Unchurched Inclusion Events' that revolve around food, hospitality and discussion.

8. Conduct 'altar calls', 'appeals', or 'opportunities' in every service for the unchurched to respond to the Gospel and/ or meet their needs through prayer.

9. Require every department in the church to conduct at least quarterly 'Unchurched Inclusion Events' that are geared specifically to attract their age/stage demographic. For example, family BBQs, youth band competitions, sports days, father-son/mother-daughter events, Kids Church 'fun days'.

10. Capitalise on all major event days as a Church. The most important days that we capitalise on for evangelism in Australia are:

- Christmas Production/Carols
- Christmas Day Service
- Easter Production/Service
- Mothers/Fathers Day with gifts and a focus on motherhood and fatherhood
- Australia Day – celebrating Australian life
- Personal Event Days where the unchurched are often prepared to be present, such as Baby Dedications, Baptisms, Weddings, Funerals (note – much skill and tact is required in making these more 'official events' attractive to the unchurched).

11. Focus on prayer for unchurched friends. Distribute the 'Prayer List' (Appendix III) among all members. When someone becomes a Christian, interview them and their church friend in a service. This keeps the church focused on the mission and purpose of your Church – winning the lost and assimilating them into your Church!
We have regularly produced "GO CARDS" so members can carry their 'prayer card' with them everywhere. It lists the names of three people that the Christian is praying for to come to Christ:

I'm Believing For...

1. _____

2. _____

3. _____

---

12. Use the following pledge to generate enthusiasm and commitment for winning the lost among the members of the church. The concept here is to teach and promote a balanced, healthy Christian life that can be sustained and made easy for every member in your church to do.

MY YEARLY PLEDGE

'DAILY'

I purpose to put God first, Thinking of Him and talking with Him in prayer, and involving Him in every decision.

'WEEKLY'

I commit myself to celebrate worship, belong to a small group, and give financially into my church.

'MONTHLY'

I will reach out in hospitality and acts of kindness to an unchurched friend.

13. Make heroes out of soul winners and those who grow the Church through introducing and assimilating new Christians into your Church family. Interview them and their friend in services, small groups and leaders meetings.

14. Preach and teach a monthly series on evangelism and witnessing at least twice a year, using different themes, topics, speakers and approaches.

The Sacred Altar Call – 'The Appeal'

In every service, without exception, we have developed the practice and expectation of conducting an 'Appeal' or 'Altar Call'. This is sacred to us. It is the personal invitation to whoever will "say yes to Jesus", and thousands have said "yes" over the years.

"Therefore we are ambassadors for Christ, as though God were making His plea through us. **We plead with you on Christ's behalf, "Be reconciled to God!"**
(2 Corinthians 5:20 NET)

THE ALTAR CALL

Making the Appeal

The following is a sample script for conducting a salvation Altar Call or Appeal. I have used this, with variations to suit the situation, over many years with great success.

It is important to script your invitation to begin with (so you don't miss any important details), make sure your approach is friendly and compelling, which will in turn cause you to be confident in your delivery.

The Appeal

"I am aware that today in this service, you may find yourself in one of three positions:

1. **"CHRIST OUTSIDE MY LIFE WITH ME ON THE THRONE OF MY LIFE, RUNNING THINGS" – "THE NATURAL MAN" (1 Corinthians 2:14)**

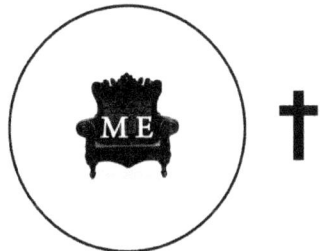

2. **"CHRIST IN MY LIFE BUT NOT ON THE THRONE OF MY LIFE WITH ME STILL RUNNING THINGS" – "THE CARNAL MAN"** (Romans 8:6-8)

3. **CHRIST IN MY LIFE AND SEATED CENTRE ON THE THRONE OF MY LIFE WITH JESUS RUNNING THINGS" – "THE SPIRITUAL MAN"** (1 Corinthians 2:12-16)

You may not have been brought up in a church, or you may have, however, what we are talking about here is your relationship with God.

The Bible teaches us that we must all **personally accept** Jesus Christ as our Saviour and Lord.

God only asks us to do two things. This is called faith. God asks to '**DECIDE**' and '**CONFESS**'.

DECIDE

I'm inviting you to personally **decide** to receive Jesus Christ as your Saviour and Lord.

There is nothing we can do to save ourselves. Jesus did everything when He died on the cross, was buried, and rose again so we could be saved.

Now He simply invites us to decide to receive His free gift of salvation.

*"But to all who have **received** him – those who believe in his name – he has given the right to become God's children." (John 1:12)*

CONFESS

The second thing that God asks us to do is to **confess** Jesus Christ as Saviour and Lord, to God and to others.

If you have decided to receive Jesus Christ as your Saviour and Lord, while every head is bowed and every eye is closed, raise your hand now and confess your decision to God and I will count it a privilege to include you in a prayer.

(after hands are acknowledged)

Thank you for your decision today… Now you are sealing the deal.

Jesus said:

*"Whoever therefore shall **confess me before men**, I will confess him also before my Father which is in heaven." (Matthew 10:32)*

This is very important because to just decide in your heart(s) and not act on your decision is simply a good idea. Public confession is part of what God asks us to do to be saved.

*"For with the **heart** man **believes** unto righteousness; and with the **mouth confession** is made unto salvation." (Romans 10:10)*

I invite you to come forward now and publicly confess your decision to accept Jesus Christ as your Saviour and Lord.

PRAYER

"Repeat this after me.

Dear Heavenly Father, thank you for loving me and sending Jesus to die for me. I now accept your free gift of eternal life in Jesus Christ.

I repent and turn from sin and everything that displeases you. Please forgive me and make me clean on the inside. Make me your child.

I promise to follow you and serve you all my life in the fellowship of your church.

AMEN"

Follow up Counselling

"Congratulations on your commitment to follow Jesus Christ! Please turn around and meet one of the leaders in our church who will chat with you and give you some material to help you become established in your new faith".

CHAPTER TEN:

ESTABLISHING THE NEW CHRISTIAN

The follow up of new Christians would be one of the most important aspects of becoming a Christian, and yet is often the greatest area of neglect by churches.

There can be many reasons for this. The simplest reason is that most follow up situations are created out of confrontational forms of evangelism, so no relationship exists. Therefore, follow up is doomed to fail.

The apostle Paul expressed his diligence in ensuring the establishing of his converts to the Thessalonians:

> *"But we were gentle among you, just as a nursing mother cherishes her own children. So affectionately longing for you, we were well pleased to impart to you not only the Gospel of God, but also our own lives, because you had become dear to us...we exhorted, and comforted and charged everyone of you, as a father does his own children."*
> *(1 Thessalonians 2:7-11)*

We have proven over the years in our church at Brisbane that a better than 90% retention rate can be achieved once new Christians are followed up effectively through the following procedure. The results are the exact opposite when follow up of the new convert is not provided.

Here are some follow up practices and procedures that we have used effectively in our church:

1. Locate the Christian friend who brought them to church, the event or small group and involve them in process… and if possible, equip them to follow their friend up.

2. If the decision to follow Christ was made during a Sunday Service or church event, a Follow Up Counsellor is assigned at the Altar Call to counsel them and to spend

time with the New Christian after the service.

Some important things to do and cover are:

- Give the new Christian helpful information such as a Bible (New Testament in modern English), information on You Version Bible apps for their phone, a booklet on their decision and information about their new Church family, showing what groups, departments and events are specially designed for them.

- Obtain personal details for the Assimilation Department.

- Cover basic scriptures on their salvation such as, forgiveness, assurance and the Christian life.

- Answer any questions.

- Pray for needs.

- Be a friend.

- Arrange a visit/connection/meeting over the next few days.

- Introduce the new Christian to at least two other members of their same age/stage and the leader of their age/stage group in the church straight after the service.

- Invite them to join an Alpha group.

From there, the Follow Up Counsellor can pass details on to the Assimilation Department so follow up can commence, involving the following procedures:

1. Phone call on Monday – within 24 hours. We have developed and trained a small team of people with

    excellent telephone and people skills to make these vital phone calls.

2.   Assimilation Leader follows up to confirm contact of New Christian and invitation to attend a small group.

3.   Assimilation Leader confirms invitation for the New Christian to attend the 'Growth Track' and 'Alpha' programs where they learn how to pray and read their Bible, about Water and Holy Spirit Baptism and how to have a relationship with God (NB. we have found that conducting these courses on a Sunday morning improves attendance and creates the habit of attending church every week).

The goals of the 'Growth Track' and 'Alpha' programs are to encourage, teach and ensure that the new Christian:

- Is born again and established in their faith in Christ

- Is baptised in the Holy Spirit and speaking in tongues

- Is baptised in water

- Is attending Church weekly

- Is a member of a small group

- Has made several friends in Church and with other new Christians

The Follow Up Contact Meeting

The physical connection with the new Christian within a few days cannot be overemphasized. This may happen in a variety of ways; at a cafe, at home or before small group that week.

The objective of this meeting is to encourage and confirm them in Christ by:

- Developing the new friendship and taking a personal interest in him/her.

- Covering key scriptures regarding their assurance of Salvation and their decision.

- Answering any questions.

- Pray with the new Christian, which in doing so shows them how to do it, and encourages them to pray.

- Asking if any of their family, friends and colleagues are interested in finding out more about their decision and offering to meet with them.

The Assimilation Department in our church tracks the progress of every new Christian for six months, giving special attention to church and small group attendance, service involvement and making sure that key discipleship steps are being made such as, attending Alpha, being water and Holy Spirit baptised, as well as regular contact by pastors and leaders of the church.

EPILOGUE:

WE HAVE TO TAP INTO THE POWER OF THE HOLY SPIRIT

"But you shall receive power, after that the Holy Spirit is come upon you: and you shall be witnesses unto me."

(Acts 1:8)

By learning the art of Holy Spirit empowered, conversational witnessing, we will be able to more effectively engage our family, friends and colleagues in a non-confrontational style of presenting the Gospel. As we do, I believe we will find more open hearts and opportunities presented to us to share our faith. This approach will lead us more to agreement rather than argument.

Additionally, this conversational style of communication would allow breathing room for us to naturally 'tap into the Holy Spirit' and become more aware of His promptings in these moments. This approach creates a more relaxed and 'normal' environment in which to tell our story, answer questions and present the Gospel of Christ.

Conversational Examples

Jesus, while engaged in a conversation with the woman of Samaria at the well, operated a 'conversational Word of Knowledge' (1 Corinthians 12:8) in the form of a question:

"Jesus said to her, Go, call your husband, and come here. The woman answered and said, I have no husband. Jesus said to her, You have well said, I have no husband: For you have had five husbands; and he who you now have is not your husband: in that you spoke truly." (John 4:16-18)

We also see Jesus arranging a meal setting in which He engages Zacchaeus in conversation and dialogue about his salvation.

Zacchaeus, hurry and come down, for today I must stay at your house." He hurried, came down, and received him joyfully." (Luke 19:5-6)

Philip the evangelist, prompted by the Holy Spirit, asked the Ethiopian Diplomat a question regarding the Scriptures he was reading while riding in his chariot:

"And the angel of the Lord spoke to Philip, saying, Arise, and go toward the south unto the way that goes down from Jerusalem to Gaza, which is desert. And he arose and went: and, behold, a man of Ethiopia, a eunuch of great authority under Candace queen of the Ethiopians, who had the charge of all her treasure, and had come to Jerusalem to worship... Then the Spirit said to Philip, "Go near, and join yourself to this chariot." And Philip ran to him, and heard him read the prophet Esaias, and said, "Do you understand what you are reading?" (Acts 8:26-30)

"You shall receive power"

In order to embrace a lifestyle approach to witnessing, we must better understand the concept of 'power' in the Scriptures.

The New Testament uses the word "dunamis', which is often interpreted to only mean 'dynamite', or explosive, dramatic, instantaneous and miraculous power. However, this is only one form of God's power.

Power can also mean 'dynamic', or strength, might, ability and influence.

This 'dynamic' power of God is what we need to tap into, so the Holy Spirit can strengthen us, enable us and cause us to have persuasion and influence as we share our story and present the Gospel of Christ to our unchurched friends, family and colleagues.

"But you shall receive power, after that the Holy Spirit is come upon you: and you shall be witnesses unto me." (Acts 1:8)

IT'S HARVEST TIME!

"Jesus said to them, "My food is to do the will of him who sent me and to accomplish his work. [35] Do you not say, 'There are yet four months, then comes the harvest'? Look, I tell you, lift up your eyes, and see that the fields are white for harvest."

(John 4:34-35)

Jesus answered them, "This is the work of God, that you believe in him (Jesus) whom he (God) has sent."

(John 6:29)

APPENDIXES

APPENDIX I – OIKOS INVENTORY

FAMILY

Name	RECEPTIVITY

FRIENDS

Name	RECEPTIVITY

APPENDIX I – OIKOS INVENTORY

WORK

Name   **RECEPTIVITY**

_____   _____

_____   _____

_____   _____

_____   _____

_____   _____

_____   _____

_____   _____

_____   _____

NEIGHBOURHOOD

Name   **RECEPTIVITY**

_____   _____

_____   _____

_____   _____

_____   _____

_____   _____

_____   _____

_____   _____

_____   _____

APPENDIX I – OIKOS INVENTORY

SCHOOL / UNIVERSITY

Name	RECEPTIVITY

APPENDIX II – PRAYER LIST

*"For God is not willing that any should perish, but
that all would come to knowledge of the truth".
(1 Timothy 1:6)*

1. _____

_____

2. _____

_____

3. _____

_____

4. _____

_____

5. _____

_____

6. _____

_____

APPENDIX III – NEW CHRISTIAN BROCHURE

YOUR PRAYER

DEAR LORD JESUS,

I COME TO YOU TODAY AND CONFESS THAT I NEED YOU. PLEASE COME INTO MY HEART JESUS.
BE MY LORD AND SAVIOUR.
THANK YOU FOR GIVING ME A BRAND NEW START.
WASH ME, CLEANSE ME AND FORGIVE ME OF ALL MY SINS. TODAY I OPEN MY LIFE TO YOU AND DECLARE "I AM SAVED".

AMEN

YOUR NEXT STEP

KNOW GOD – GET CONNECTED
DISCOVER PURPOSE – MAKE A DIFFERENCE

'DAILY'
I purpose to put God first in my every day through prayer and reading the Bible.

'WEEKLY'
I commit to actively being involved in attending church services and groups.

'MONTHLY'
I will reach out in hospitality and acts of kindness to others.

NEXT STEPS | NEW CHRISTIANS

NAME

PHONE

EMAIL

DOB

FIRST TIME DECISION ☐ REDEDICATION ☐

HAVE YOU BEEN WATER BAPTISED?

HAVE YOU BEEN FILLED WITH THE HOLY SPIRIT?

WHO ARE YOU CONNECTED WITH AT CHURCH?

TAKE YOUR NEXT STEP

☐ I WOULD LIKE TO ATTEND ALPHA

☐ I WOULD LIKE TO START THE GROWTH TRACK

☐ I WOULD LIKE TO GET CONNECTED IN A GROUP

Your privacy is important to us. Your details will only be used for the purpose of communication with you about C3 Church events and programs. You can obtain a copy of our privacy policy via our website.

BIBLIOGRAPHY

Aldrich, J. "Lifestyle Evangleism", Sisters, Oregon, Questar Publishers, 1981.

Am, W., and McGavran, D., "How To Grow a Church", Glendale, California, Regal Books, 1973.

Kaldor, P., "Build My Church (NCLS)", Sydney, Australia, Open Book, 1996.

Kaldor, P. "Winds Of Change (NCLS)", Sydney, Australia, Open Book, 1996.

Schuller, R.H., "Your Church has Real Possibilites", Glendale, California, Regal Books, 1974.

Wagner, C.P., "Your Church can Grow", Ventura, California, Regal Books, 1976.

White, J., "Flirting With The World", Wheaton, lIlinoise, Harold Shaw Publishers, 1982.

McCrindle Research. (2017, May 19). Faith & Belief in Australia. Retrieved from http://faithandbelief.org.au/wp-content/uploads/2017/05/Faith-and-Belief-in-Australia-Report_McCrindle_2017.pdf